Material World

MATERIALS TECHNOLOGY

Robert Snedden

H www.heinemann.co.uk
Visit our website to find out more information about Heinemann Library books.

To order:
☎ Phone 44 (0) 1865 888066
▤ Send a fax to 44 (0) 1865 314091
▢ Visit the Heinemann Bookshop at www.heinemann.co.uk to browse our catalogue and order online.

First published in Great Britain by Heinemann Library,
Halley Court, Jordan Hill, Oxford OX2 8EJ
a division of Reed Educational and Professional Publishing Ltd.
Heinemann is a registered trademark of Reed Educational & Professional Publishing Ltd.

OXFORD MELBOURNE AUCKLAND
JOHANNESBURG BLANTYRE GABORONE
IBADAN PORTSMOUTH (NH) USA CHICAGO

Designed by Celia Floyd
Originated by Dot Gradations
Printed by Wing King Tong, Hong Kong

ISBN 0 431 12103 6
05 04 03 02 01
10 9 8 7 6 5 4 3 2 1

British Library Cataloguing in Publication Data

Snedden, Robert
  Materials technology. - (Material world)
  1.Materials science - Juvenile literature
  I.Title
  620.1'1

Acknowledgements
The Publishers would like to thank the following for permission to reproduce photographs: Ancient Art and Architecture: p13; Andrew Lambert: p21; FLPA: B Borrell p4; Nutan/Rapho/Network p11; Sally and Richard Greenhill: p14; Science Photo Library: Martyn F Chillmaid p6, Martin Bond p8, David Parker p9, Chris Knapton p15, Harvey Pincis p16, Maximilian Stock p17, James Stevenson p18, Tek Image p19, James Holmes/Thompson Laboratories p24, NASA pp26, 27, Peter Menzel p29; Tony Stone Images: Chris Shinn p5, Ross Harrison Koty p12, Keith Wood p23, Wayne Eastep p25

Cover photograph reproduced with permission of Tony Stone Images: Mark Segal

Every effort has been made to contact copyright holders of any material reproduced in this book. Any omissions will be rectified in subsequent printings if notice is given to the Publisher.

Any words appearing in the text in bold, **like this**, are explained in the glossary.

Contents

Making materials

Material like wood requires little processing other than cutting into the desired shape.

One definition of materials is that they are substances from which we make things. The materials we use can be split into two groups: natural materials and extracted materials. Natural materials, such as stone, wood and wool, can be used almost as they are found in nature, and require little more than shaping and cleaning. Extracted materials, such as plastics, metals and **ceramics**, have to be created from other **raw materials** or separated from other materials before they can be used.

With tried and trusted materials that have been used for a long time, such as iron and concrete, the method of production may not have changed over many years. Other materials appear through accidental discovery or as a result of painstaking research in the laboratory.

Manufacturers decide which material to use for a particular job by looking at the properties of different materials. For example, copper wires are excellent at conducting electricity, whereas long strands of sheep's wool are not. On the other hand, a jumper knitted from copper wire might not be very comfortable.

Materials science

The job of the materials scientist is to study the relationships between the way materials are put together and the properties they have. Some properties of a material can be seen straight away – it does not take long to discover that wood floats but rocks do not. However, it may take more careful examination to discover why this is so. Rocks are generally made of tightly packed **crystals**, making them relatively **dense**. The low density of wood is due to the open structure of the once-living **cells** that it is made of. This kind of detail only becomes visible when the materials are examined through a microscope.

Materials engineering

Materials engineering deals with the structure, properties, production and uses of various materials. Materials engineers can either try to find new and improved ways of using existing materials or they can try to develop new materials to meet changing needs. Working together, materials scientists and engineers have developed a huge range of materials to meet the changing needs of our complex societies. These range from the waterproof yet breathable fabrics used in outdoor clothing to the strong but lightweight **alloys** of titanium used for aircraft parts.

Extracting the materials we need from the ground often has undesirable consequences such as damage to the landscape.

One thing is certain – the job of the materials scientist will never be done because we will always want to make new things. It's simply human nature.

The right materials for the job

It is vitally important to match the materials used to the job they have to do. For example, the strength of the materials used in bridge building needs careful consideration as it would be disastrous if they failed.

Properties of materials

The properties of materials can be divided into various groups, such as their mechanical, chemical and electrical properties.

Mechanical properties

Mechanics deals with objects in motion and the forces acting on them. Mechanical properties are important in a wide variety of structures and objects, ranging from guitar strings to rocket engines. Some of the most important mechanical properties of materials are stiffness, resistance to stress, toughness and strength.

The stiffness of a material determines how much it will bend when a force acts on it. For example, it would be a bad idea to make shelves of rubber as they would bend alarmingly whenever anything was put on them.

Stress is a force acting on a material that will change its shape. Materials that do not resist stress and change shape readily, such as modelling clay, have limited uses.

Stress tests are carried out to determine how well a material will stand up to the demands placed on it.

Toughness measures a material's resistance to cracking. The tougher the material, the greater the stress necessary to break that material near a crack.

The strength of a material tells us how great a force can act on a material without it breaking. A material's strength depends on many factors, including its toughness and its shape.

Chemical properties

The chemical properties of a material include such things as its resistance to **corrosion**. For example, iron has to be protected from rusting, which occurs when it reacts with oxygen in the air.

Electrical properties

Electrical properties are important in materials designed to carry electric **currents**, or to block them. The copper wires inside a plug are good **conductors** of electricity, while the plug's plastic casing is good at blocking it.

Try it yourself

You will need
a selection of everyday items such as a piece of wood, an old plate, an empty tin, a piece of brick, an empty plastic drinks bottle (please check with an adult before using these items)
a chopping board
a cloth
a hammer
SAFETY: Always have an adult to supervise this activity

1 Put an item on the chopping board and cover it with the cloth.
   WARNING: always cover the item with a cloth in order to protect your eyes!
2 Give the item a sharp blow with the hammer. What happens to it? Does it bend or break? Does it crack? Does it resist the blow entirely? Try this with all your items.

Superconductors

If a material is cooled to a very low temperature its **electrical resistance** drops off to practically zero. This is called **superconductivity**. Scientists are searching for materials that are superconducting at everyday temperatures. Materials such as this could transform our lives. Electricity flowing through superconducting power lines could reach homes and industries without any loss of energy. Computers with superconducting components would be much more powerful, and more compact, than anything we have today.

High-speed trains could speed through the countryside propelled by powerful, pollution free superconductor-generated magnetic fields.

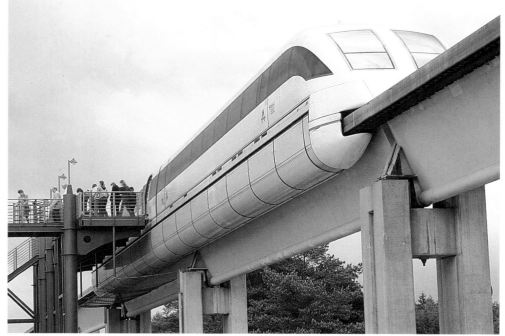

The first superconductor

*The first **superconductor** was discovered in the Netherlands, in 1911, by Heike Kamerlingh-Onnes, a physicist who studied the properties of materials at extremely low temperatures. He chilled mercury, measuring the metal's electrical resistance as he did so. He found that the mercury's resistance decreased steadily until, at about four degrees above absolute zero, it suddenly vanished entirely. Other metals behaved in the same way, but because cooling the materials to these temperatures was expensive no practical use could be found for superconductors.*

It just keeps going and going and ...

In one experiment physicists connected batteries to superconductors, then removed the batteries from the circuit. The **current** continued to flow as if the batteries were still in place. It was still flowing four years later when the scientists took the circuit apart. It is believed that a superconducting current could last millions of times longer than the universe has existed.

High-temperature superconducting

If scientists could create materials that are superconducting at room temperature, efficient delivery of energy and magnetically levitated high-speed trains could become a reality. The closest found so far are the high critical temperature, or Tc, superconductors. These copper oxide **ceramics** were discovered in 1986 and are far more practical than metal **alloy** superconductors as they do not need to be quite so cold to work. These new materials became superconducting at higher temperatures which is the same as −49°C. It is still very cold but it means that the superconductors can be chilled much more easily using liquid nitrogen, which is cheap and easy to produce, rather than liquid helium.

Scientists at Los Alamos National Laboratory in the United States made wires from yttrium-barium-copper-oxide that could carry more than 1000 times as much current as a typical household copper wire. Unfortunately the wire is only 5 centimetres long, but the team hope to make it longer.

A magnet floats above a superconducting disc. The magnetic field is expelled from the disc when it becomes superconducting.

Polymers

A polymer is a large molecule that is formed by linking many smaller **molecules** together into a long chain. These smaller molecule building blocks are called **monomers** and there may be thousands making up a polymer chain. The process by which monomers are linked together to form a polymer is called polymerization.

The first synthetic polymer was bakelite, produced in the United States in 1909 by Leo Hendrik Baekeland. In the 1930s nylon became the first **fibre** to be made entirely from chemicals in the laboratory. Since then more and more uses have been found for polymers.

This form of polymerization is called condensation polymerization because it is accompanied by the removal of water as the monomers join together.

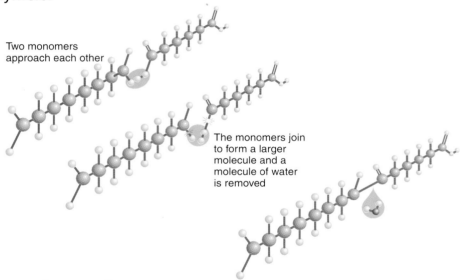

Two monomers approach each other

The monomers join to form a larger molecule and a molecule of water is removed

Everyday polymers

We probably encounter polymers every day. Starch, found in many foods such as potatoes and rice, is a polymer formed by plants from glucose (a simple sugar). Polyethylene, a tough plastic material that has many uses, is an example of a synthetic polymer that has been created in the laboratory.

The great length of a polymer chain gives the molecule many useful properties. For example, polymers do not dissolve easily because of the large size of the molecule chains. Rubber is a polymer that occurs both naturally and is also made artificially. It can be stretched to many times its original length without breaking because the polymer chains simply straighten out as it is pulled and then curl back up again.

Composite materials

Composites are produced by combining two or more separate ingredients while keeping the properties of each ingredient. Some materials are very strong when made in the form of fibres. Brittle materials such as glass, for example, can be produced without any cracks that would weaken them. Fibreglass is a composite material made by setting glass fibres in a polymer. Products made using this material include boats, sports equipment and car parts.

Carbon fibres, like any other fibres, have limited use as they can only be made into rope-like shapes. Carbon-reinforced plastic is made from strong, lightweight carbon fibres set inside an artificial polymer. Combining the carbon fibres with a polymer allows manufacturers to produce strong, lightweight materials in almost any shape.

Fibreglass can be used to make strong, lightweight hulls for boats.

Alloys

Many pure metals are too soft or rust too easily to be very useful. Often they can be made more useful by combining them with other **elements** to form an **alloy**. Alloys have been developed to do a variety of jobs, such as making strong but lightweight aircraft bodies; tough, hardwearing drill bits; and for parts in computer technology. Most alloys are stronger and harder than the pure metals from which they are made, but they are more difficult to hammer into shape, roll into sheets or draw into wires. Most have lower melting points than pure metals.

An alloy always consists of two or more elements, at least one of which is a metal. Alloys usually contain a large amount of one metal, called the base metal, combined with smaller amounts of other materials. These materials can be either other metals or nonmetals, such as carbon or silicon. Alloys are usually made by melting the base metal and then adding the other materials to it. Three, four or more different substances may be present in a single alloy.

Types of alloy

Aluminium is a common base metal for alloys that have to be strong but light. Mixed with small amounts of copper, manganese and magnesium, pure aluminium produces alloys that are as strong as steel and only slightly heavier than the pure metal. Aluminium alloys are used to make drinks cans and bicycle parts among other things.

Magnesium is another useful base metal. Aircraft and car parts are made using magnesium alloys. Titanium alloys are very strong and light, and are used to make jet engines and tough, resistant equipment for **chemical plants**.

The first alloys

People first discovered alloys in prehistoric times. The first alloy made by people was bronze, which was first produced accidentally around 3500BC. The oldest bronzes were mixtures of copper and arsenic. Over the next few hundred years, it was discovered that a more useful bronze could be made by mixing tin with copper. Bronze is much harder than pure copper, and it is easier to melt and cast into useful shapes. It was used to make tools and weapons.

Iron and steel

Iron is the most important metal for industry. It is almost always used as an alloy rather than as a pure metal. The most widely used iron alloys are the steels. All steels contain small amounts of carbon and manganese and large amounts of iron, but they vary in composition.

- Carbon steels are the most widely used steels. Their strength and durability give them a wide range of uses such as in construction, car manufacture and for food storage.
- Alloy steels contain nickel, chromium, and molybdenum. These are very strong and are used to make bicycle frames and aircraft landing gear.
- Stainless steels contain chromium, and many varieties also use nickel. Stainless steels resist **corrosion** very well and are commonly used in medical equipment and kitchen utensils.

Bronze was the first alloy to be discovered and was soon being used to make tools and weapons.

Ceramics

Ceramics are materials that require high temperatures to be manufactured. Most ceramics are hard and resistant to heat and chemicals. These properties give them a variety of uses in industry. Ceramics include everyday materials such as bricks, cement and glass and more unusual materials used in electronics and spacecraft.

Common ceramics are made from **minerals** called silicates, such as clay, silica and talc. Chemists make materials called advanced ceramics in the laboratory from **compounds** such as silicon carbide and barium titanate. Most ceramic products can withstand attack by acids, gases, water, salts and high temperatures.

Making ceramics

The clays and other minerals used in ceramics are dug from the earth and **refined** to remove impurities. The materials are then crushed and ground into fine **particles**, and the correct amounts of each are mixed together. Water or another liquid is added to produce a mixture that can be shaped. Glass and some heat-resistant ceramics are made by melting the particles and shaping them while they are molten.

Ceramics are fired in furnaces called kilns. This process hardens the ceramics and gives them great strength.

After the product has dried, it is strengthened by firing. This is done in special **furnaces** called kilns. Ceramics are fired at temperatures ranging from about 650 to 1650°C. Firing hardens the product permanently and gives it strength and durability. Many ceramic products are covered with a glassy coating called a glaze. This gives the ceramic a smoother surface and makes it waterproof. Glazes are also used for decoration.

Heat-resistant ceramics called refractories are used in the manufacture of industrial boilers and furnaces, such as those used to make steel. The tiles that cover the surface of space shuttles are refractories that can withstand the intense heat created by re-entry into the Earth's atmosphere at high speed. Ceramic materials used in making refractories include magnesium oxide, silica, silicon carbide and zirconium oxide.

Ceramics have excellent insulating properties and are often used as insulators on high voltage power lines.

Ceramic products

The properties of ceramics make them especially suitable for certain products. Some extremely hard ceramic materials, such as silicon carbide, are used for cutting metals and for grinding, polishing and sanding various surfaces. Clay and shale are used to make strong, durable ceramic bricks and drainpipes for buildings. Baths, sinks and toilets are made of porcelain, which is made mainly from clay, feldspar and quartz. Because ceramics are resistant to chemicals, do not absorb liquids and are not harmed by sudden changes in temperature they make excellent containers for food and drinks. Most ceramic tableware is made from a mixture of clays, feldspar and quartz.

Common ceramics such as porcelain are poor **conductors** of electricity and this property makes them good **insulators**. They are used as insulators in spark plugs, on electricity power lines and in electrical equipment such as television sets. Another ceramic material is used in making **capacitors**, which store electric charges in electronic equipment. Magnetic ceramics are used in electronic circuits and in electric motors.

Glass

It would be hard to imagine life without glass. It is used to make containers for storing drinks and other containers, called glasses, from which to drink them. It is used to make lenses for telescopes, microscopes and spectacles. Light comes into our homes, schools and work places through glass windows. Glass **fibres** can be used to make tough materials for building or stretched out over long distances to carry electronic communications.

Glass is a first-class storage material; easy to make, unreactive and transparent so you can see what's inside!

How to make glass

*No one knows when or where people first learned how to make glass. The first manufactured glass is believed to have taken the form of a glaze on **ceramic** vessels, some time in the 3000s BC. The first glass vessels were produced about 1500 BC in Egypt and Mesopotamia.*

*A large amount of silica sand and small amounts of soda ash and limestone are mixed together. Other materials such as aluminium oxide, sodium sulphate and lead oxide may be added to give the glass special qualities. The mixture is heated in a **furnace** until it forms a syrupy mass. The mixture will melt at 1427°C to 1593°C, depending on its composition. On cooling, it becomes glass.*

Types of glass

When you think of glass you might at first think of a clear, hard material that is easily broken. However, there are many different kinds of glass, with different uses.

Glass-ceramics

These very strong materials are made by heating glass so that its **atoms** fall into regular patterns like **crystals**. Glass-ceramics are resistant to chemicals and can withstand high temperatures and sudden changes in temperature. They have a wide range of uses, from cookware to the nose cones of guided missiles.

Laminated safety glass

Laminated safety glass is made from layers of plastic material and flat glass. The outside glass layer may break if something strikes it but the inner plastic layer stretches and holds the broken pieces of glass together, and so prevents them from flying in all directions. It is used for car windscreens. Bullet-proof glass is made from several layers of laminated glass.

Tempered safety glass

Tempered safety glass looks like ordinary glass and weighs the same. It is a single piece of glass that has been given a special heat treatment. It can be five times as strong as ordinary glass and will resist even a blow from a hammer. If it does break, it collapses into small, dull-edged fragments. It is used widely for glass doors in shops.

Grinding a telescope lens takes patience and skill to make sure it has no flaws.

Glass fibres

Fibreglass manufacture was first developed in the 1930s. Each fibre is a very thin solid rod of glass. Glass fibres can be loosely packed together to form an **insulating material** that can be used in electrical insulation and fire-resistant materials. Thin, extremely pure optical fibres can transmit telephone and television signals over long distances.

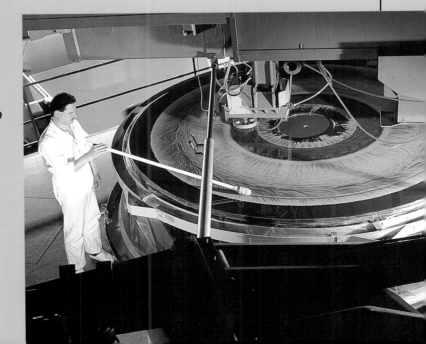

The chemical industry

The chemical industry plays a vital role in the production of many manufactured goods. It takes **raw materials** such as oil and gas and uses chemical reactions to transform them into useful materials that can be put to work for a variety of different purposes. Paper products, flavourings for food and drink and plastics are all products of the chemical industry.

In a chemical plant raw materials are transformed into useful products on a large scale.

The industry also provides a tremendous variety of raw materials to be used in various processes by manufacturers. Most of the chemicals produced are used in the manufacture of other products. Sulphuric acid is produced in huge quantities and is used to make **fertilizers**, paints, explosives and numerous other chemicals.

Chemical engineering

Chemical engineering deals with the large-scale production of chemicals and chemical products. Chemical engineers are concerned with the chemical processes that change raw materials into useful products. They plan, design, and help to construct **chemical plants** and equipment. They develop efficient and economical ways of producing chemicals such as cosmetics, drugs, fertilizers and plastics.

The success of the chemical industry has brought environmental and safety problems with it. Many of the processes involve handling and transporting large quantities of sometimes hazardous chemicals. They also produce a great deal of unwanted waste material that has to be disposed of safely to avoid polluting the environment.

Try it out for size

Once chemical engineers have checked that there are no safety risks the building of a chemical plant can begin. The choice of a place to build is also important. The raw materials needed for the chemical process need to be readily available and the finished products have to be transported quickly to where they are needed. Both of these things have to be taken into account to keep costs down.

Teamwork

The chemical engineer works with mechanical, industrial and electrical engineers who also have a part to play in the safe and efficient design of plants and equipment. Environmental engineers are involved in making sure that the hazardous by-products of chemical processing are safely disposed of. Most chemical companies also employ people to work on research and development of new substances, and finding ways to make more use of known chemicals.

Many of the materials and products of the chemical industry are highly dangerous if they are not handled carefully.

Materials and food

Many materials are used in the production and storage of food: chemicals are used to preserve it; metal, paper and plastics are used for storage; and additives such as colourings and flavourings are used to make food look and taste better. Technologists are always looking for ways to improve these methods.

Food preservatives

One of the oldest methods of food preservation is curing. This involves adding ingredients such as salt, spices, sugar and sodium nitrite to food. It is widely used in preserving some meat products as well as fish, potatoes, cucumbers and certain nuts. Curing ingredients may be rubbed on to the food or applied by soaking the food in a solution of the ingredients. Some meat and fish are cured by smoking. Wood smoke contains chemicals that slow the growth of **micro-organisms**.

Canning

In the canning process foods are sealed in airtight containers and then heated to destroy micro-organisms that may cause spoilage. A wide variety of foods can be preserved in this way, including fruits, fish and poultry. One of the disadvantages of canning is that the heat required for **sterilization** changes the food's texture, colour and flavour. Also, some **nutrients** are lost in the canning process. Often colourings, flavourings and vitamins are added to put some of these things back.

Canning food can help to preserve it for a longer period of time.

Additives

Additives are chemicals added to foods to prevent spoilage, improve appearance or to increase nutrients. There are hundreds of different additives. Some additives, such as antioxidants and preservatives, help keep foods edible for as long as possible. Many foods contain **compounds** that combine with oxygen and change into new compounds that may be harmful, or have an unpleasant smell or taste. Antioxidants prevent this from happening. Preservatives, such as salt, stop micro-organisms growing in foods. Preservatives are used in foods that cannot be canned or frozen, such as bread and cheese.

Flavouring agents can be natural, such as spices and fruit juices, as well as artificial flavour enhancers, such as monosodium glutamate (MSG) which is made from vegetable protein. Natural sweeteners such as sucrose and glucose may be added to food to make it taste sweeter, as can artificial sweeteners such as aspartame and saccharin.

Oranger oranges

Colouring agents are often added to make foods look appealing. Orange colouring agents are often added to the skins of oranges to improve their appearance. Colours are used a great deal in the manufacture of sweets.

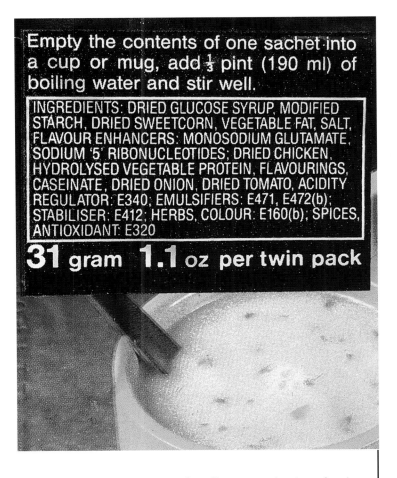

Empty the contents of one sachet into a cup or mug, add ⅓ pint (190 ml) of boiling water and stir well.

INGREDIENTS: DRIED GLUCOSE SYRUP, MODIFIED STARCH, DRIED SWEETCORN, VEGETABLE FAT, SALT, FLAVOUR ENHANCERS: MONOSODIUM GLUTAMATE, SODIUM '5' RIBONUCLEOTIDES; DRIED CHICKEN, HYDROLYSED VEGETABLE PROTEIN, FLAVOURINGS, CASEINATE, DRIED ONION, DRIED TOMATO, ACIDITY REGULATOR: E340; EMULSIFIERS: E471, E472(b); STABILISER: E412; HERBS, COLOUR: E160(b); SPICES, ANTIOXIDANT: E320

31 gram 1.1 oz per twin pack

Additives are used to flavour and colour food as well as helping to preserve it.

Medical materials

The branch of medicine that is concerned with making artificial parts for the body is called prosthetics. An artificial part, called a **prosthesis**, does the job of a body part that has been lost or damaged as the result of injury, disease or a birth defect. Some types of prostheses are used inside the body. For example, damaged hip joints can be replaced by artificial ones made of metal or plastic. Artificial heart valves can be used to replace faulty ones to help people with heart problems. Some mechanical devices are used to do the job of a body part without actually replacing it, such as a pacemaker that keeps the beating of the heart steady. A dialysis machine does the work of the kidneys, but lies outside the body.

Although artificial limbs are not as good as the real thing they are of great benefit to many people.

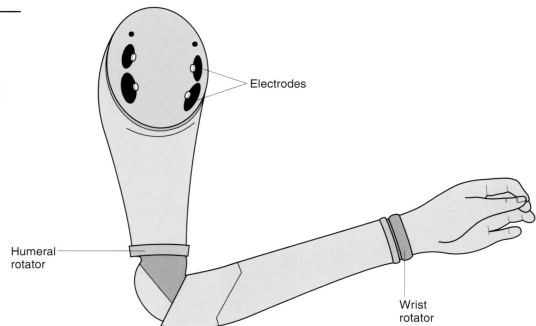

Electrodes

Humeral rotator

Wrist rotator

Biomedical engineering

Biomedical engineers use engineering skills to solve problems in biology and medicine. Some biomedical engineers design medical instruments for monitoring, diagnosing and treating diseases. Others test different materials to find which are the most suitable for use as artificial body parts.

The right materials

Selecting the right materials to place inside the human body is a very important task. The biomedical engineer has to understand how the body works, especially the properties of that part of the body that will be replaced by the new material. It is vital that the new material should cause no harmful effects in the body. At the same time, the body's defences have to be considered as they could damage a material and so stop the new body part from doing its job. A replacement body part should ideally last a lifetime. Materials that are suitable for these purposes include certain **ceramics**, metal **alloys** and plastics.

Chemists

Many of the medicines we use are made from materials found in the natural world. For example, several important medicines are obtained from plants and **moulds**. The **antibiotic** penicillin comes from a mould, for example. Pharmaceutical companies produce several common drugs from **minerals**. Iodine, for example, is used in making tincture of iodine, a liquid that helps prevent infection when applied to cuts.

Pharmaceutical firms are continually trying to develop new and more effective drugs. Creating a new drug is the task of a company's research chemists. They may find a new drug from a natural source or they might make a new chemical **compound** in the laboratory.

Chemists carry out tests on a variety of materials in the search for new medicines.

Materials on the farm

Many farmers today rely heavily on the chemical industry to provide the **fertilizers** they need to produce crops and the **food supplements** needed to raise large herds of animals, as well as chemicals to combat pests.

Fertilizers

If crops are grown in densely planted fields the amount of **nutrients** and water they require for healthy growth may be greater than nature can provide. Farmers may send samples of their soil to a soil-testing laboratory to learn which nutrients may need to be added. Most crops need large amounts of nitrogen, phosphorus and potassium, and so most commercial fertilizers are made up mainly of these elements, but chemical companies can provide fertilizers for almost any crop requirement.

Pesticides

Most farmers control pests with chemicals called **pesticides**. There are hundreds of pesticides, each one designed to combat a certain type of weed, plant disease or harmful insect. Pesticides can be hazardous if misused. They can pollute the environment, threatening animals and plants other than pests, or get into the food supply and so be a danger to human health. For these reasons their use has to be carefully monitored.

Farmers can send samples of soil to the laboratory for testing to discover if it is low in any nutrients.

Organic farming

Organic farming relies on natural substances rather than on manufactured chemicals to fertilize the soil and control pests. Manure (animal waste) is the most widely used organic fertilizer. However, most specialized crop farms have few animals or perhaps none at all and cannot produce enough manure to provide the fertilizer their plants need.

Many farmers spray their crops with pesticides to combat insects – there is always a risk that these chemicals will harm other animals as well.

Try it yourself

You will need
moist gardening sand
two seed trays
plant fertilizer
some seeds, such as broad beans

1 Fill each tray with 3 or 4cm of sand. Add a little fertilizer to the sand in one of the trays.
2 Plant a few seeds in each tray making sure they are well covered.
3 Put the trays in a warm, well-lit place. Be sure to check the trays often and keep them moist.
4 After a few days the seeds should sprout into seedlings. Watch how they grow. Do you see any difference between the seedlings growing in the sand and those grown with fertilizer?

Materials in space

Several important factors have to be considered when choosing materials to build a spacecraft. The materials used include **ceramics**, metals, polymers, **semiconductors**, **composites**, adhesives, lubricants and paints. Weight is an important consideration. The heavier the craft the more fuel it will need to get into space and so the more expensive it will be to launch it. Because of this, honeycomb structured panels of aluminium metal **alloy** are used – these give great strength but weigh relatively little.

The materials chosen have to last a long time too. A satellite could have a useful life of up to 30 years but it is rather tricky to replace a part that wears out. There are great extremes of temperature in space as an orbiting satellite, travelling around the Earth, moves in and out of the sunlight. The spacecraft designer has to know how much the materials used will expand and contract as they are heated and then cool again. Protective thermal blankets can reflect heat away from parts of the spacecraft facing the Sun, while at the same time they store heat to prevent parts pointing away from the Sun from getting too cold. The spacecraft also has to be resistant to **radiation**. In space there is no atmosphere to protect against the Sun's ultraviolet light. Polymers, especially, can be damaged by this radiation.

Building space stations in orbit around the Earth requires the use of many lightweight and durable materials.

Alloys in space

Materials scientists are developing many new alloys that provide greater strength and durability than has ever been achieved before. These superalloys are made from the metals nickel or cobalt, to which chromium and a variety of other materials are added. They can resist extremely high temperatures and exposure to highly corrosive chemicals. The superalloys will be used in spacecraft construction and in high performance jet aircraft.

Space mining

As well as taking materials into space, we might one day get materials from space. If frozen water is found in the deep craters on the Moon, for example, it would mean that the basic gases for rocket fuel (hydrogen and oxygen), oxygen for life support and construction materials for colonies could all be supplied. This would avoid the huge cost of shipping everything from Earth.

Many asteroids are thought to be the remains of comets and may also contain water ice, so they too could be tapped for the hydrogen and oxygen used to make rocket fuel. Asteroids are also believed to contain huge amounts of pure iron, nickel, cobalt, platinum and even gold. Even the smallest known metallic asteroid contains several times more metal than the total amount that has been mined and processed in all of human history. If the history of humanity is to continue in space we have to learn how to make use of the resources to be found there.

Space scientists are already planning to send an unmanned probe to an asteroid that will bring a rock sample back to Earth.

Materials in the microworld

Using devices such as the **atomic force microscope**, scientists can now directly push **atoms** and **molecules** about and prod them into place. Researchers have already made a **transistor** out of a single carbon molecule and some people believe that microscopic **nanorobots**, able to push atoms and molecules together, could be used to produce a wide range of essential materials. Huge numbers of these nanorobots would supply materials at almost no cost, wiping out hunger and ending pollution from conventional factories.

What is nanotechnology?

A nanometre is one billionth of a metre (about three or four atoms wide). Nanotechnology is about working on this scale. It means building things, one atom or molecule at a time, and placing them exactly where we want them. Nanotechnology uses the known properties of atoms and molecules to produce materials of astonishing perfection. Nanotechnology would allow us to build materials that have extraordinary properties, such as completely flawless metals that would be much stronger than anything we have today. It could mean a huge step forward in technology, including supercomputers no bigger than human cells and spacecraft that are no more expensive to build than family cars.

A molecular machine – you!

If you want to see a nanotechnology machine, just look in the mirror. Proteins are molecular machines that routinely move individual atoms around. If you eat a banana, for example, proteins in your body take it apart, use some of it for energy and reassemble some of it as

Smart materials

Not happy with the colour of your room? Imagine if you could simply touch the walls and command the smart nano-liquid covering them to produce a rainbow of colours until you found one you liked. The nano-liquid could be laced with nano-computers – you might paint a tiny computer screen on your thumbnail, or a videophone on the palm of your hand.

parts of you. Scientists have begun to design proteins in the laboratory that can perform particular tasks. A customized protein might be placed on the tip of an **atomic resolution microscope** where it could take a specific molecule out of a chemical **solution** and move it to the right place to form part of a nanotechnology machine.

Microrobots

Most items we want to use are made of trillions of atoms. It would take a long time to make anything useful one atom at a time. The first aim of nanotechnology is to produce a nanorobot that can make copies of itself. This assembler robot could make copies and those copies could make copies. Soon trillions of assemblers controlled by nano-supercomputers would be assembling objects at a phenomenal speed.

When will it happen?

Some nanotechnologists believe that these wonderful machines could be with us in ten to fifteen years time. However, the problems to be solved are immense. How would you write a computer program that could control the activities of a billion microscopic robots so they all worked together to produce just what you wanted? There may be a gap of many years between the construction of the first assembler robot and the first 'miracle' products rolling off the microassembly line.

It is hoped that in the future robot insects will be able to perform repairs inside otherwise inaccessible machinery.

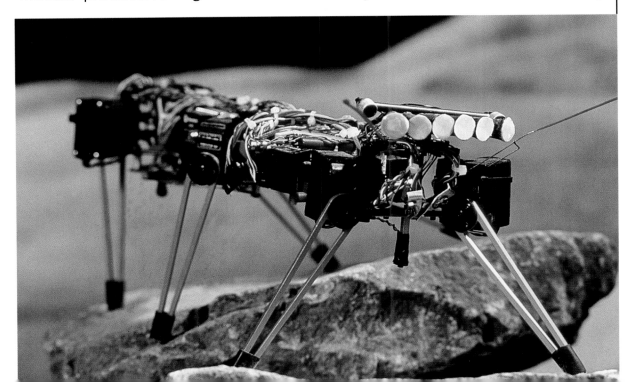

Glossary

alloy a mixture of two or more metals or a metal and a non-metal

antibiotic a substance produced by or obtained from certain bacteria or fungi that can be used to kill or inhibit the growth of disease-causing micro-organisms

asteroid one of a number of large rocky, metallic objects that orbit the sun; also called minor planets, the largest is over 900km across

atomic force microscope a microscope that produces an image by dragging a diamond probe over the surface of an object to map the shape of its surface. The up and down movements of the tip are converted into images on a screen. The tip may be a single atom.

atomic resolution microscope a microscope, such as the atomic force microscope, that can resolve images on the scale of atoms

atoms tiny particles from which all materials are made; the smallest part of an element that can exist

capacitor a device for storing an electric charge, used in electronic circuits

cells the basic units of life. Cells can exist as independent lifeforms, such as micro-organisms, or form tissues in more complicated lifeforms, such as muscle tissue in animals.

ceramics non-metallic solids that stay hard when heated

chemical plant factory where chemicals are produced on an industrial scale

comet large frozen ball of gas, ice and dust, like a giant dirty snowball, that travels around the sun

composites materials designed by combining other materials with properties that go well together

compounds substances made up of atoms of two or more elements

conductors substances through which heat or electricity can be transmitted

corrosion the eating away of metals by chemicals; rusting is a type of corrosion

crystals solids in which the atoms or molecules making it up are arranged in orderly patterns

current a flow of something, such as a liquid, gas or electric charge

dense density is a measure of the compactness of a substance

electrical resistance a measure of how much a material resists the flow of electricity through it

elements substances that cannot be broken down into simpler substances by chemical reactions, an element is made up of just one type of atom

fertilizers chemicals added to soil to provide nutrients for plant growth

fibres long continuous filaments or threads of a material

food supplements minerals or vitamins added to food

furnace a chamber in which materials can be heated to a very high temperature

insulating material a material that blocks the flow of electricity or of heat

insulators materials that block the flow of electricity or heat

micro-organisms living things too small to be seen with the naked eye

minerals naturally occurring solid substances; substances obtained by mining

molecule two or more atoms combined together; if the atoms are the same it is an element, if they are different it is a compound

monomers chemical compound composed of simple molecules from which polymers can be made by joining the monomers together

moulds types of fungus

nutrients substances that are essential for the maintenance of life

particles tiny portions of matter

pesticides chemicals used to kill insects and other pests

that damage crops and livestock

prosthesis an artificial replacement for a damaged or missing body part

radiation high energy rays or particles given off by radioactive atoms as they decay

raw materials materials used in the manufacture of something

refined having had any impurities removed

semiconductors materials used in electronic circuits that have an ability to conduct electricity somewhere between that of metals and insulators

solution a mixture of one substance dissolved in another

sterilization the killing or removal of living organisms, especially disease-causing bacteria and other micro-organisms

stress a force acting on an object that changes its shape

superconductivity the increase in a material's ability to conduct electricity at very low temperatures when its electrical resistance becomes practically zero

superconductors materials that show superconductivity

transistors components in an electronics circuit used to regulate the flow of current

Index